HOW TO STUDY EFFECTIVELY

BY

GUY MONTROSE WHIPPLE

PROFESSOR OF EDUCATION
UNIVERSITY OF ILLINOIS

Author of "Manual of Mental and Physical Tests," "A Guide to High-School Observation," "Questions on General and Educational Psychology," "Questions in School Hygiene," etc.

PUBLIC-SCHOOL PUBLISHING CO.
Bloomington, Illinois

INTRODUCTORY

Not long ago I was asked by a group of high-school students to present to them some suggestions on the technique of studying, with the idea that better knowledge of the methods by which school work could be prepared might increase their efficiency as students. A survey of the available literature seemed to warrant the conclusion that, despite the existence of a number of books upon the art of study, there was still room for another treatment that should be limited to the direct laying down of a series of rules or maxims, with just sufficient explanatory comment to make them readily intelligible and serviceable for the needs of the average high-school or college student. I judge that many students in our high schools and colleges are not now working under the best possible conditions, and that they would be glad to increase their efficiency, if only they knew how to do it. The rules which follow are intended to help these students. Most of the suggestions could also be profitably kept in mind by elementary-school teachers, whose business it should be as early as possible to develop right habits of study in their pupils.

3

While it is true that much of what is presented in the school is calculated to appeal directly to the native interests of students, to elicit their curiosity, and to challenge their attention, it is equally true that most studying is real work, and that most boys and girls have to acquire the art of studying as they have to acquire many other habits and skills necessary to success in life. Moreover, conditions in many elementary schools are unfortunately such as to promote only the most superficial kind of studying, to put a premium upon the mere committing to memory of words, to permit fickle and ill-sustained attention and the avoidance of hard intellectual-work. Students in both high school and college have been studying, it is true, for years, but too often they have not been studying efficiently, have not formed right habits of mental work, and indeed, do not even know how to go about the development of an adequate method or plan for such work. They are often unable to recognize as such the problems set before them, nor do they have clear ideas as to the methods by which problems should be solved. Neither do they know fully how to deal with those 'lessons' that must be 'learned' more or less verbatim. For by 'studying' I mean to include the 'getting of lessons,' like learning a list of words in spelling, as well as studying in the sense of solving problems and making an investigatory examination and critical survey of a topic.

In what follows I propose no universal remedy for these ills. The fundamental differences between stupid children and bright children will remain whether they are taught to study or not. No scheme of instruction will bring all students to the same level of proficiency. But the proficiency of each student may be increased by teaching him to use more skillfully what brains he has. Thus, Breslich*, for example, shows that a weak section studying only at school, but under careful supervision, may be brought up to the performance of a strong section allowed to study at school without supervision, plus an hour and a quarter a day at home. Granting that these results are typical, how much time must have been wasted in the studying of the strong pupils?

Efficiency is the watch-word of modern industrial life. The school, after all, is a sort of brain factory. Its material is found in the subject-matter of the various studies and in the mental operations of its students. Studying is the method by which subject-matter is converted into ideas that shall be effective in the subsequent life of the students and by which at the same time the mental capacities of the students shall be drilled and trained. It is safe to say that failure to guide and direct study is the weak point in the whole educational machine. There is more than a fanciful analogy in the parallel between scientific management in modern industry and control of the technique of study in the modern school. The elimination of 'waste motion' in the

---

*See *Suggestions For Further Reading*, appended to the text, for references to books and articles dealing with studying.

factory must be paralleled by the elimination of 'waste motion' in the school. The chief source of this waste lies in the process of studying.

THE RULES

1. Keep yourself in good physical condition.

Your mental efficiency depends on the efficiency of your central nervous system. This system suffers like any other part of your body from inadequate exercise, insufficient sleep, ill-digested food, or confinement in ill-ventilated rooms.

Sleep. More students sleep too little than sleep too much. From the averages of the six best authorities we may recommend the following duration of sleep:

Age	6	7	8	9	10	11	12	13	14	15	16	17
Hours	12.3	11.5	11.2	11.0	10.5	10.2	9.8	9.6	9.25	9.0	8.75	8.5

Exercise. Remember that exercise, particularly in the form of outdoor recreation and games, is valuable not merely for requiring strength, and skill, but also for stimulating the digestive, circulatory, and excretory systems of the body to the more active supplying of nutrition and removal of waste products. Further, that exercise carried on under pleasant auspices affords a useful antidote for mental weariness and monotony.

2. Attend to, remove or treat physical defects that often handicap mental activity, such as defective eyesight, defective hearing, defective teeth, adenoids, obstructed nasal breathing.

Vision: Thirty per cent. of school children have defective vision. In high school and college the percentage is larger. Consult a competent oculist if you have difficulty in seeing clearly objects at a distance (like writing on the blackboard) or if you experience, eye ache, twitching of the eyelids, inflamed lids, headache, nervous irritability, nervous dyspepsia and similar symptoms of eye-strain, after use of the eyes at close range, even though you see the printed page quite clearly.

Defective teeth seriously affect the work of students, because (a) the mastication of food is inadequate; (b) the neglected cavities afford a breeding ground for scores of varieties of bacteria (including the germs of serious infectious diseases, like diphtheria and tuberculosis); (c) the pus which develops often finds its way into the blood and alimentary canal and thus pours into the body millions of noxious germs and produces general bodily ailments, like intestinal catarrh, anemia, lowered vitality and other general disturbances which appear to be in no way connected with the local disturbances in the teeth; (d) the pain of toothache acts directly to distract attention and indirectly to induce various reflex nervous irritations. When we consider that one or more defective teeth are found in 90 per cent. of school children, the total loss of efficiency in school work attributable to this single cause is truly startling.

Adenoids are enlargements of spongy tissue in the upper part of the throat just where the nasal passages open into it. They are found in some ten per cent. of school children, particularly of children from 3 to 16 years of age. They interfere with breathing, clog the Eustachian tube and thus induce hardness of hearing, mouth-breathing, snoring, projecting teeth, stunted bodily growth and imperfect development of the bones of the nose and jaw. In some persons they cause a peculiar sort of mental sluggishness, or stupidity, with inability to control and direct attention for long to a difficult mental task. They can be removed by a relatively simple operation and with marvelously beneficial results to both mind and body.

3. See that external conditions of work—light, temperature, humidity, clothing, chair, desk, etc., are favorable to study.

A quiet place for work that shall be reasonably free from interruption and from distracting conversation is greatly to be desired. Too many students have to do their home work under conditions that are far from ideal. Study, at least when it is begun, demands active attention. In order to get attention upon work, it must be withdrawn from other matters. Every happening in the room in which you are working makes a claim for your attention. A portion of the energy you exert in attending to your work has to be expended to shut out these distracting claims. Clearly, then, if you can work in a room in which these outside appeals are reduced to the minimum, you will gain that more energy to devote to your tasks.

As you get older, your capacity to direct all your energies upon your mental work, even against distraction, ought to increase. A profound philosopher in the midst of his meditations would never notice the little noises and movements that immediately distract the attention of the kindergarten child. However, the difference between the child and the philosopher is largely one of degree— of how much gunpowder, as some one has expressed it, would have to be exploded under his chair to wreck his train of thought. This getting used to distractions is a good thing to acquire, but still there are usually enough of them without deliberately placing yourself in conditions that will increase their number.

Light should never shine directly into your eyes. Don't face a window or brightly lighted wall. Don't let an artificial light hang in the immediate range of your eyes unless they are protected by an eye-shade or by a suitable shade on the lamp. Nor should the illumination be so directed as to be reflected directly from paper or books into your eyes. The direction of illumination should be predominantly from above and for desk work from a point to the front of, and to the left of, your body, in order that shadows shall not be cast on your work by your head or by your hand (in right-handed persons). For reading, when the book is held in the hands, the light may be placed above and somewhat behind, whether on the right or left is then indifferent. An ideal illumination for desk work at night may be secured by a single small electric lamp (perhaps 8 candle-power) under an opaque reflector, arranged to flood the desk with light, but to be itself invisible to your eye. The cutting off of illumination from the remainder of the room is restful and assists, by lessening distractions, in concentrating attention upon the work before you.

A **temperature** between 65 and 68 degrees is conceded to be favorable to most workers. Beyond 70 degrees, particularly under artificial heating, flushing of the face, headache and other signs of discomfort are apt to appear. This discomfort is usually more a consequence of low **humidity** than of high temperature. In the winter, therefore, any sort of device that will add moisture to the air (evaporation from pans of water over furnace or on steam or hot-water radiators, etc.) will lessen the dryness of the indoor air (often exceeding that of the Desert of Sahara) and comfort the skin and mucous membranes of the body. Recent experimental studies show also that the keeping of air in motion by fans will remove the discomfort felt in ill-ventilated rooms to an extent not usually dreamed of.

Tight clothing, particularly tight neckwear, interferes with mental work directly by its discomfort and indirectly by impeding respiration and circulation. A tight collar checks the flow of venous blood from the head and tends toward flushing the face and increasing blood pressure in the eyes and the brain.

The study desk and chair should be of a height to fit your needs. Too low a desk encourages stoop-shoulders, a contracted chest and a congested head. Too high a desk is uncomfortable for your arms and brings the work too near your eyes. A little experimenting, especially with the height of the chair relative to the desk, will often make a wonderful difference in the comfort with which study can proceed.

The equipment of your desk should be such as to bring the various 'tools' of study conveniently before you. Have these 'tools' of study (pencils, erasers, ruler, pen and ink, blotters, dictionaries, drawing sets, pads of paper and the like) in good condition and so placed as to be at hand when wanted, but out of the way when not wanted. High-school and college students who can afford it ought to buy a typewriter, have a simple stand for it, and do as much of their work as possible upon it. A rack that will hold heavy books, like dictionaries used in translation work, at a reading angle of 45 degrees is another useful desk device.

4. Form a place-study habit.

Have a particular place—a particular desk, a particular chair—at which you study. Do your studying there unless special conditions warrant doing it elsewhere. At least, don't permit yourself to do anything but work at this particular place. Don't ever loaf or read novels or newspapers in the chair dedicated to study. This advice may strike you as a bit far-fetched. By no means. Once get this place-study habit formed and you have only to take your place to start up the studying attitude.

5. Form a time-study habit.

When school work follows a regular schedule there can be discovered a natural sohedule for studying. For most persons there is a real advantage in doing mental work by schedule, in setting aside given periods for study and in following this schedule rather closely. For one thing, you are not likely then to get behind in your work. And again, a tendency appears to be developed in the nervous system of turning to mental work at times ingrained by habit.

Whether this time-study habit should be more *specific*, so that a particular subject is studied at a given day and hour (geometry, daily at 11; Latin, Monday, Wednesday and Friday at 8 p. m.) is open to question. I doubt that the nervous system can be trained to habits of working with particular subjects at particular hours. However, many students are convinced that such a plan is valuable because of the advantages of pursuing daily work methodically, of laying out a program and sticking to it.

Whether, again, different people are by nature so constituted as in general to do mental work best at different portions of the day, so that A is a "morning worker," B an "afternoon worker," C an "evening worker," is also open to question. Habit would appear to play a considerable role here. I think that most evening workers could become morning workers if they had to. Several of the writer's friends think they do creative and constructive work better late in the evening and 'hack' work better in the day time. By preference they would write an essay at night and revise it in the morning.

6. When possible prepare the advance assignments in a given subject directly after the day's recitation in it.

This is a special case under Rule 5: "Form a time-study habit." The reasons for it are these: (a) The mind is 'set' or 'tuned up' for the particular subject; there is a special fitness for work in physiology or history or whatever the work may have been, and this 'swing' should be utilized.* (b) The assignment for the work to follow is fresh in mind. (c) The study of a given topic is separated from the recitation on that topic by an interval—probably twenty-three hours or more. As is explained below (Rule 25) two impressions of a given material are more effective for permanent memory when separated by an interval. It follows that the transposed order—study x, then at once recite x, which is so much favored by students on account of the benefit of 'recency'—cannot be recommended for the best permanent results.

7. Begin work promptly.

Observation of high-school students† shows that

---

*There is little danger of loss of 'swing' through being bored. The actual material studied will be different from that dealt with in the recitation.
†See Breslich, Reference 1, page 105.

even when they know that only a short period is available for studying a given lesson, nearly every one is slow to start. Some of them take ten or fifteen minutes to go through the motions of getting started. Here is a woeful waste of time. Get before yourself the ideal of a quick 'get-away.' Reduce your starting time from minutes to seconds. One help to this is to:

8. Take on the attitude of attention.

Get your materials laid out before you. Take your pen or pencil. Sit up straight. Open your book. Carry out all the 'motions' of getting to work. If you have drilled yourself well, this will be enough to start you to work. The beginning is often the hardest point; once begun, you can keep on without much effort.

9. Work intensely while you work: Concentrate.

You are not likely to remember what you deal with half-heartedly. Vivid impressions are most lasting. Ideas flow most rapidly when you work 'at white heat.' Put as much 'steam' into your work as into your play. Don't dawdle. When E. B. Andrews was President of Brown University he used one phrase in his Chapel prayers that might well voice the attitude of all good students: "Help us to apply ourselves with unremitting assiduity." Note, too, that this means be attentive in class as well as in your home work.

10. But don't let intense application become fluster or worry.

You can be intent without being anxious, earnest without being flustered. There is a kind of hurry that "defeats its own end." In especial, don't worry because you can't keep pace with the best student in your class. No two of us are alike. Do your best and admit your limitations if others learn faster, recite more readily and secure higher marks.

11. Do your work with the intent to learn and to remember.

Laboratory experiments with memorizing under different conditions show very clearly that one of the most important conditions of good memory is the taking of the attitude of 'intent to remember' when the materials to be learned are presented. Closely allied with this is the attitude of 'confidence' in one's ability to remember what one is learning. An illustration may be seen in the following incident. I once had occasion to read aloud a list of words to a student enough times so that he could recite them correctly. I repeated the process with a second and with a third student. I then discovered to my amazement that I was unable to recite the list by heart myself. Here not only the most charitable, but also the psychologically correct explanation, is that I never *intended* to learn the list myself. I had repeated it mechanically and not in the memorizing attitude.

12. Seek a motive or, better, several motives.

Some school subjects are intrinsically interesting. You would rather study them than not. Without urging you find them interesting. But other subjects, or even the favored subjects under certain conditions, are not intrinsically interesting. If attention is given to them, it is because a motive or incentive is found that can be attached to them. Among the most obvious incentives are recognition of the value of the subject to you in the future, anxiety not to fail in anything you undertake, longing to be a credit to your parents, resolve to 'get your money's worth' out of your investment in schooling, ambition to beat your classmates, to beat your own previous record, to maintain a good reputation, competition for grades, prizes, honors, sense of duty, love of the approval of teachers, parents and friends, necessity of graduating to get a better start in life, fear of various penalties, etc. Our motives are mixed, some are remote, others immediate. Some of them are felt to be higher and worthier than others. The fundamental point is that to do your best work, you need strong incentive. Skillful teachers know how to develop and appeal to many motives, but you can help yourself by deliberately seeking for motives for your own work. Moreover, many a task begun under artificial compulsion comes in time to be itself directly attractive.

13. Get rid of the idea that you are working for the teacher.

The teacher's real function is to supply the materials, guide your application and test your performance, not for the teacher's sake, but for your sake. Remember that you are really working for yourself when you are studying.

Whoever watches students in the preparation of their tasks must be struck with the extent to which the form and quality of their work is dictated by the attitude and demands of the teacher of each subject. Miss X insists on neat papers and gets them. Miss Y insists that all references shall be looked up, and they are looked up. Mr. Z. is found to be keen on the knowledge of idioms, and they are known in his class, though his references may not be looked up nor his papers rendered in neat form. Admittedly, you can hardly be blamed for thus controlling your work in some measure through motives of expediency: your immediate object is to get good grades. What I urge is that beyond these lesser details you should see clearly that in the larger view your work is, after all, primarily done for yourself, not for your teachers.

14. Don't apply for help until you have to.

Don't give up the problem after the first failure to solve it, but "try, try again." You learn by your own effort and progress through your own failures.

It is the teacher's province, of course, to give aid to students, but the best aid to mature students comes through suggestions, hints, queries—"Where do you think the trouble lies?" "Have you tried this method?" "Do you see any connection between this problem and that?" "Read over such and such a page again," etc.

15. Have a clear notion of the aim.

Understand definitely what the task is—not merely how many examples or pages or lines of translation you are to do, but what the purpose of the assignment is, by what methods you are supposed to work, what aspects of the lesson are salient and essential, what things, if any, should be learned verbatim, what you should 'look up' outside the textbook—in short, what this particular piece of work is for. Naturally, it is the teacher's business to be sure this aim is made clear in assigning the lesson. Unfortunately, too little attention is paid by many teachers to steering the student's work on the coming lessons.

16. Before beginning the advance work, review rapidly the previous lesson.

The reasons for this rule are fairly obvious. (a) The subject-matter is familiar and hence not difficult to attend to. Your work starts off easily. (b) The reviewing is directly useful to deepen the impression of the reviewed material. It aids you greatly in recalling that material later on. (c) The mental activity used in the reviewing serves to 'warm up' your mental processes for the studying to follow. (d) The subject-matter thus reviewed will have numerous points of contact, numerous 'hooks' upon which the new material can be fastened. The reviewing helps, in other words to "associate the new to the old," which is one of the most fundamental maxims in all learning.

17. Next make a rapid preliminary survey of the assigned material.

This rule is not applicable to all subjects, but for work in language, history, geography, physiology and the like, and even in most forms of mathematics, this preliminary canter over the ground gives a useful notion of the 'lay-out' of the whole task and frequently economizes time otherwise lost in the earlier part of the lesson in struggling over points that are explained in the later part. The preliminary survey also helps to hold the material together in a more unitary whole. It should never, of course, replace the careful study that is to follow: it is only preliminary to that.

18. Find out by trial whether you succeed better by beginning with the hardest or with the easiest task when you are confronted with several tasks of unequal difficulty.

Individuals differ in this respect. Many find that anticipation of the more pleasurable, easier task to follow lightens the more difficult and less pleasurable task. It is a distinct satisfaction to say: "There, that's done, now for something easier." Others, especially those who 'warm up' slowly and do their best work only after they have been mentally active for a period, can probably defer the harder task to some advantage. A lengthy stint with portions of unequal difficulty can be done then by 'cleaning up' the easier portions first and then making a final spurt for the remainder.

19. In general, use in your studying the form of activity that will later be demanded when the material is used.

You will use your knowledge of spelling ninety-nine times in a hundred in the writing of words in sentences. In accordance, then, with this rule it would be better to learn your spelling by writing the words than by learning them merely orally; in fact, it would probably be still better to learn them by writing them in actual sentences than to learn them merely by writing them in lists or columns. Young pupils need to know their multiplication tables for use in actual arithmetical work: it follows that these tables will be really learned only when they can be used in actual problems. Teachers are often surprised to discover that pupils who have learned the multiplication tables fairly well as tables still cannot multiply rapidly and accurately when they try to solve examples. Again, conversational French or German is to be employed presumably in talking: let it be learned aloud, then, rather than by silently perusing a textbook or by writing dozens of French or German sentences from dictation. Similarly, students who sometimes complain that they "know that stuff but can't answer questions on it" would do well to do their reviewing of it by asking themselves questions about it and practising the giving of answers.

20. Give most time and attention to the weak points in your knowledge or technique.

This rule seems almost too obvious to mention,

yet it is one that is frequently infringed against, because human nature takes most satisfaction in doing what is easiest. Thus, most children in taking piano lessons spend their time in playing over and over simple 'pieces' that they have already learned to do fairly well, but have to be constantly urged to devote time to the fingering of difficult runs and to the important exercises with scales. In school work, similarly, teachers and texts often devote too much time to what is easy: the child has as much drill in "two times two are four" as he does in "eight times seven are fifty-six," despite the fact that the latter connection is probably several dozen times more difficult to master. Mature students are competent enough to detect their own weaknesses and to seek by special exercises to fortify themselves at these points. If your translation of German is interfered with by irregular verbs, spend an extra half-hour a day for several weeks on the conjugation of these verbs. If your exercises in physics come out wrong because of mistakes in arithmetic, take the trouble to remedy this defect by special practice in number work.

21. Carry the learning of all important items beyond the point necessary for immediate recall.

Adequate learning means permanent acquisition. Any bit of information that is needed for your life work must be studied more than is sufficient barely to recall it for the purposes of tomorrow's recitation next month's examination. Remember that all impressions tend to fade with time and that this fading must be met by **overlearning**. If the process of extracting a square-root needs to be perfectly ready for use at the age of forty, it must be drilled upon in the grammar grades far longer than is necessary just to keep it in mind during the work in the grammar-school arithmetic. Superficial learning of spelling may answer for the immediate test, but is totally inadequate if the aim is to get the process so automatic that all words in common use can be written at any time in your life correctly and without hesitation. From this it follows:

22. You must daily pass judgment as to the degree of importance of items that are brought before you, and lay special stress on the permanent fixing of those items that are vital and fundamental.

Naturally, young children are in no position to make these decisions. It is the business of their teachers to accentuate these essential points and by suitable emphasis and repetition to insure their mastery. But many high-school and most college students are mature enough to appraise the items of knowledge and to select for careful learning those that are valuable for them. These items might as well be learned once for all when they appear.

At the same time, this rule does not mean that the thousands of less fundamental items are not to be thoroughly understood and attentively mastered as they are encountered. The prospect that ten years after you graduate you will be unable to recall the third person, singular subjunctive of *amo* or to give a clear statement of Avogadro's hypothesis or to demonstrate that the sum of the angles of a triangle is equal to two right angles does not prove that you would better not spend time on them now. If all the time and energy we spend studying the thousands of facts that we are afterwards unable to recall were time and energy thrown away, education would be, indeed, a most ridiculous farce! In reality, knowledge once known but not now recallable is by no means valueless.

(a) It may have had an immediate direct usefulness when learned, sufficient to justify learning it, using it for a time and then forgetting it. I take a quarter of an hour to learn the main streets and the general system of transportation in London, though I expect to be there only one week in my life.

(b) Much of what we learn has value primarily as preliminary instruction. It furnishes the temporary scaffolding by means of which the permanent structure may be laid. No doubt Latin, properly taught, improves English composition, oral and written. At thirty you will have forgotten your Latin grammar, but you will probably speak better English for having done the Latin translation for which the grammar prepared you.

(c) Somewhat similarly, in order to understand and to retain permanently the larger generalizations, it is necessary to assimilate a considerable number of the detailed observations on which the generalizations are built. Put quantitatively, one might say that to make ten principles one's own, one must first acquire knowledge of a hundred or a thousand concrete facts and illustrations. These examples will be forgotten, but they will have done their work by guaranteeing the memory of the principles behind them. The particular experiences combine to form a valuable mental acquisition.

(d) Knowledge once learned and now forgotten can be re-learned in far less time than the original learning. Some part, then, of the original labor is still conserved in the nervous system, even though actual recall is impossible.

(e) The original labor of learning has taught you where to go to get information of certain kinds and by what methods to get it.

It would not, therefore, be entirely ridiculous if a well-trained man were to boast: "I have forgotten ten times as much as you ever knew!"

23. When a given bit of information is clearly of subordinate importance and useful only for the time being, you are warranted in giving to it only sufficient attention to hold it over the time in question.

Contrary, then, to the notions of many teachers, 'cramming' or reliance on 'recency' is sometimes perfectly legitimate. No lawyer has all his legal lore 'on tap' perpetually. No clergyman knows at every moment in his life all the details of theology and scriptural exegesis that he pours forth so fluently from Sabbath to Sabbath. No engineer could elaborate a new bridge without 'sweating up' on those phases of bridge designing that pertain to his new problem. In so far, then, as the school aims to train for life, it may properly seek to train this ability to cram.

24. Make the duration of your periods of study long enough to utilize 'warming-up,' but not so long as to suffer from weariness or fatigue.

However successful you may become in making a prompt start (Rule 7), you are likely to be in a better 'swing' after five or ten minutes than after two minutes. It would be unwise, therefore, to cut short your work at the end of ten or fifteen minutes unless the task were extremely hard, you were extremely tired and you had come to a natural break in the work. Easy work, especially when the task is changing from minute to minute, can often be continued profitably for two hours or more with little interruption. Hard work, with quick onset of weariness, is best interrupted oftener, say every fifteen or twenty minutes, by short breaks, say of one minute, made at points that afford natural stopping places. Walk about a bit. Open the window. Get a brief change and relaxation, but do not do other mental work.

It is impossible, then, to lay down any hard and fast rule concerning optimal length of study, save to say: (a) the maturer the student, the longer he should be able to work; (b) the easier the subject matter, the longer he should be able to work; (c) the slower the student is to get 'warmed up,' the

longer he should continue at work. A special case
is indicated in the following rule:

**25. When drill or repetition is necessary, distrib-
ute over more than one period the time given to a
specified learning.**

It is not possible to state just precisely what is the
best possible way to distribute the time to be devoted to learning (so much depends upon the various conditions of work as indicated in Rule 24).
Obviously, a small task that can be learned in a few
minutes had better be learned in one sitting. Obviously, a difficult task requiring, say four or five
hours of labor, had better be learned in several sittings. The present rule means that, in general, the
work of studying is more economical and efficient
when a given amount of time is divided into several
sittings than when it is taken in a single sitting.
Experiments show, for example, that more rapid
progress is made in learning to typewrite if the
practice is in two periods of thirty minutes each,
separated by a day, than if the practice is all undertaken in one period of sixty minutes. Similarly, a
piece of piano music that can be learned by heart
in a single sitting of 120 minutes can be learned
equally well in less than 120 minutes if taken in
sittings of 15, 20 or 30 minutes each, separated by
intervals of several hours or days. Especially in
the case of college work, where conditions often
favor deferring application to certain courses until
a forth-coming 'quiz' compels extensive reading and
reviewing, there is an undoubted loss of efficiency,

because the same amount of labor expended in shorter and more frequent periods of study would ensure considerably greater permanence of the material. The distributed learnings can be undertaken with less fatigue, with less fluster and worry. Moreover, it is probable that during the intervals between these learnings some sort of 'organization' or 'incubation' of the material takes place. Many persons find it profitable, for instance, to assemble data for a paper or essay several days before they attempt to write it, as experience shows that these data 'come out' in better shape for having been allowed to 'stand' for a time.

26. **When you interrupt work, not only stop at a natural break, but also leave a cue for its quick resumption.**

This is peculiarly important when undertaking a relatively long bit of constructive work, like writing an essay. At the moment you stop, you have fairly clearly in mind the general perspective of your task. What you have done is fresh before you; what you propose to do is more or less already in outline. Everyone knows how 'cold' and even distasteful such a piece of work can be when it is picked up after a day or two devoted to other matters. To remedy this, jot down memoranda before you leave it: "Start next a discussion of so-and-so." "Pick up point on page 4 for further treatment." "Look up this and that in the encyclopedia," etc.

27. After intensive application, especially to new material, pause for a time and let your mind lie fallow before taking up anything else.

The impressions just made are liable to be blurred or 'swamped' by the second set, unless they have a little time to settle down. It is a matter of common experience that the details of a day spent in sight-seeing in an environment full of novel impressions, your first day at a World's Fair, for example, are peculiarly hard to remember. I once urged a German friend who was visiting America for the first time to meet some colleagues at my home in the evening. He declined courteously on the ground that he had just spent a busy day in an intensive study of the George Junior Republic and that unless he could spend a quiet evening at the hotel, he would not carry home with him a clear memory of the institution he had just visited. His attitude was quite correct. His evening at the hotel would suffice to arrange his impressions, to fix them indelibly in his memory, unobscured by other impressions of a different sort. He would spend his time, of course, in thinking over what he had seen and heard during the day. This brings us to a particularly important set of rules.

28. Use various devices to compel yourself to think over your work.

The function of the recitation is to induce thought as well as to 'hear lessons.' Examinations have as one function the incitement through the reviewing in preparation for them of a comprehensive survey of the ground covered by them.

Certain plans for inducing thinking are sufficiently important to be embodied as specific rules.

29. Form the habit of working out your own concrete examples of all general rules and principles.

This rule is applicable more particularly to the work of students in college and in the upper years of the high school where the subject-matter of study is more apt to deal with abstract and generalized statements. A good textbook or a good teacher will be sure to supply one or more concrete examples of such general principles, but the good student should supplement these by examples of his own. The point is that your personal experience is different from that of the author of the text or from that of the teacher. If, then, you really understand the principle you are studying, it is probable that some illustration of it will occur to you that is different from the one given you, and quite likely better than that one for your own purposes. Teachers who have real insight will always give more credit for a student's own attempt to apply a principle, even if it be a crude one, than for a mere parrot-like repetition of the illustration made in the text or the classroom instruction.

30. Form the habit of mentally reviewing every paragraph as soon as you have read it.

A properly constructed paragraph centers about one thought which may usually be epitomized in a single sentence or even a single phrase. Make sure that you can 'tease out' this thought. This habit of mental summarizing by paragraphs might well be developed by teachers in the grade schools.

31. Don't hesitate to mark up your own books to make these essential ideas stand out visibly.

The marking may take the form of underlining or side-heads may be written against each paragraph. It is well to do this after reading each paragraph. The decision what to mark or what to write will necessitate thinking out the gist of the paragraph. The text is also left in better shape for subsequent reviewing by topics. Naturally, this advice suggests that each student should own as many texts and reference books as possible.

32. Whenever your desire is to master material that is at all extensive and complex, make an outline of it. If you also wish to retain this material, commit your outline to memory.

It has often amused me to see the eagerness with which college students scan the pages of the 'patent' books on memory which advertise to teach one the secret of "how to master the contents of books at a single reading," and how sadly they greet the advice: "Read the book carefully, make an outline of it and memorize the outline." Nevertheless, this is perfectly sound advice, psychologically and pedagogically, for there is "no royal road to learning."

The outlines should be much condensed, preferably in noun-form statements, topics, catch-words and phrases rather than full sentences, and the most careful attention should be paid to their organization under main headings, sub-headings, etc. The idea is to get from the reading of a chapter or an essay or an argument the framework of the whole structure and to set this down on paper in a form that reveals its organization in a glance.*

33. In all your work apply your knowledge as much as possible and as soon as possible.

There is scarcely any rule more fundamental than this one. To be sure to remember a thing, do something with it, try it, use it, put it into function, tell it to some one, go to almost any length to express what has been impressed upon you. All teachers know that they reach most complete appreciation and permanent retention of any topic when they have had occasion to teach it to others. The astounding grasp displayed by men in the learned professions over the thousands of intricate details of their callings is a consequence of the constant use they are making of these materials. Even so trivial an issue as the remembering of some good story is best met by telling the story to some one as soon as possible after hearing it or reading it. An excellent plan for any student who is anxious to master any topic is to seek to explain it to another person.

In this connection the query may be raised: Does group studying operate to increase the effectiveness of the individual student's work? The answer must

---

*Students of law, debating, argumentation and the like will find described in J. H. WIGMORE, *Principles of Judicial Proof* (Part III., pp. 744 on) a very interesting and valuable plan for charting in visible form the details of a mass of evidence.

be: "It depends." In certain high schools experiments with a form of group work applied to the studying of history, civil government and the like, under the direction of the teachers, have been decidedly successful.* When students, outside of school hours and without supervision, combine in the preparation of their assignments, the results may be good, provided the students in question are more or less of the same grade of ability, and provided they take pains to share the labor in such a manner that each one of them continues to participate in the several aspects of the assignment. The tendency that too often develops within such voluntary groups for a few of the students to do the work and pass it over to their weaker brothers or for the several tasks to be delegated, so that one student looks up the vocabulary, another keeps watch on the grammar, a third makes a rough translation and a fourth polishes it off for the group, is plainly an undesirable tendency. If group studying brings about a real and active discussion of the material of the assignment with interchange of opinion and argumentation, the result is highly beneficial and contributes to the efficiency of all members of the group by putting their knowledge into use as advised in the rule given above.

34. Do not hesitate to commit to memory verbatim such materials as definitions of technical terms,

---

*See, for instance, LOTTA A. CLARK. Group work in the high school. *Elem. School Teacher*, 7: 1907, 355-444. Also C. B. SHAW. Some experiments in group work. *Ibid.*, 329-334.

formulas, dates and outlines, always provided, of course, that you also understand them.

Younger students are apt to commit their 'lessons' to memory and to recite parrot-like, in the exact words of the textbooks. The efforts of teachers are frequently expended, and quite wisely, too, in breaking up this habit or at least in ensuring that these students surely know the meaning of what is reproduced in this fashion. On the other hand, older students may make the mistake of avoiding entirely reliance upon rote memory. You should understand that committing to memory is perfectly legitimate when the subject-matter has but few natural cues for recall (as is the case with many formulas and dates) or when the subject-matter condenses into brief compass certain fundamentally important principles (as is the case with definitions and rules of procedure). You should aim to understand this material, but you should also take the pains to commit it to memory by the simple process of attentive repetition.

35. When the material to be learned by heart presents no obvious rational associations, it is perfectly legitimate to invent some artificial scheme for learning and recalling it.

An artificial scheme of this sort is termed a mnemonic device. To take a stock instance, I remember that the volcano of Fujiyama in Japan is 12,365 feet high by dwelling on the circumstance that this number embraces the twelve months and 365 days of the year. To avoid getting the wrong volcano I might even concoct some far-fetched association between *Fujiyama* and *fugitive year*. Or, again, I remember that a certain infant used sixteen words at the age of one year by recalling the proverb "speech is silver," etc., and that Bryan's speech on the silver question argued for "16 to 1!" It may be pointed out that most of the books of patent recipes for memorizing err in urging the use of such artificial devices when a rational association, a logical connection, would be preferable. Thus, the scheme that they recommend of learning vocabularies by the insertion of artificial connecting links has little to recommend it. You can, to be sure, learn that *tree* is the translation of the Latin *arbor* by saying to yourself: "*tree* suggests *mast*; *mast* suggests *ship*; *ship* suggests *harbor* and *harbor* suggests *arbor.*" But it would be far wiser for you to dwell on the fact that "Arbor Day" is a day devoted to tree planting and that our "arboreal ancestors" were the apes who lived in trees. In any event, if you must use a mnemonic device, invent your own rather than adopt a second-hand one: you are less likely to forget it on account of the very effort that you make in constructing it.

36. In committing to memory a poem, declamation or oration, do not break it up into parts but learn it as a whole.

In other words, read it straight through from beginning to end, then repeat this until the whole can be said without error. The advantages of this method are several. (a) The mental connections formed between the words are distributed evenly over the entire material, whereas, when the learning is 'by parts,' certain portions, say the first line, are repeated many more times than is necessary, while other portions, say the connection between the eighth and ninth lines, are not impressed as many times, so that forgetting appears at these weak links in the chain of associations. (b) It is easier to keep attention upon the material when it is read as a whole than when a small bit of it is repeated monotonously over and over. (c) The impressions made of any given section follow each other after a longer interval when learning is by wholes and thus there is a gain in efficiency in accordance with the principle stated in Rule 25. (d) The meaning of the material is kept to the front when it is learned as a whole, and this aids in its retention.

In case there is in the selection a portion that offers special difficulty in learning, the rule just given should be modified to the extent of devoting a few extra, short repetitions to this harder section in order to bring it up on a level with the remainder.

You may feel discouraged when you first use the method of committing to memory 'by wholes,' because, after you have expended some time upon the work, you find yourself unable to repeat any considerable part of it, but you must remember that the entire selection is already partly impressed and that when recall does become possible, it will pertain to the whole selection. The gain by the 'whole' method is greater when the selection is a long one.

even so long as to take more than a single sitting
for a single perusal.

**37. In committing to memory, it is better to read
aloud than to read silently and better to read rapidly than slowly.**

Attention is probably better sustained when the
reading is aloud, and in addition an appeal is then
made directly to the ear as well as to the eye, and
some assistance is given by the 'feel' of the words
in the throat and mouth.

There is a gain by fast repetition only in the sense
that, given a specified time for learning, a fast rate
will be advantageous by permitting you to repeat
the material more times. Thus, if you can read
through a poem slowly in five minutes, more learning will result by doubling the rate and thus reading it through twice in five minutes.

**38. If your work includes attendance at lectures,
take a moderate amount of notes during the lectures, use a system of abbreviations, and rewrite
these notes daily, amplified into a reasonably compendious outline, organized as suggested in Rule 32.**

College students are seen to err in both directions
in taking notes. Those who scribble away indus-
triously throughout the hour undoubtedly take
down too much and on the whole lose something
of the lecturer's presentation. On the other hand,
the few students who take no notes, because they
think they can do better by giving undivided attention to the lecturer's presentation, are equally de-

ceived, for no person can carry away and retain permanently the essential features of a typical lecture, without memoranda to which he can refer subsequently for study and review.

Since the taking of notes and memoranda of reading in reference books, class discussions, etc., is an activity that will be prominent in the daily work of most secondary-school and college students, some simple system for recording the commonest words and for systematically abbreviating other words might profitably be taught to all high-school students. A single symbol should be used for all common particles, like *in, on, of, with, to, tion, ing, which, that,* etc. Make up a system for yourself.

You will actually gain time in the long run if you will take the pains daily to go over the notes secured in class and at least to revise them, if you do not rewrite them completely. This work enables you to scrutinize your memoranda while they are still 'warm,' to make such alterations and additions as will increase their serviceability in the future, and, what is equally important, it serves in itself as a valuable second learning, separated from the first impression by a suitable interval (Rule 25) and consequently peculiarly valuable in assuring permanent retention.

SUMMARY OF THE RULES

1. Keep yourself in good physical condition.

2. Attend to, remove or treat physical defects that often handicap mental activity, such as defective eyesight, defective hearing, defective teeth, adenoids, obstructed nasal breathing.

3. See that external conditions of work (light, temperature, humidity, clothing, chair, desk, etc.) are favorable to study.

4. Form a place-study habit.

5. Form a time-study habit.

6. When possible, prepare the advance assignment in a given subject directly after the day's recitation in it.

7. Begin work promptly.

8. Take on the attitude of attention.

9. Work intensely while you work: Concentrate.

10. But don't let intense application become fluster or worry.

11. Do your work with the intent to learn and to remember.

12. Seek a motive or, better, several motives.

13. Get rid of the idea that you are working for the teacher.

14. Don't apply for help until you have to.

15. Have a clear notion of the aim.

16. Before beginning the advance work, review rapidly the previous lesson.

17. Make a rapid preliminary survey of the assigned material.

18. Find out by trial whether you succeed better by beginning with the hardest or with the easiest task when you are confronted with several tasks of unequal difficulty.

19. In general, use in your studying the form of activity that will later be demanded when the material is used.

20. Give most time and attention to the weak points in your knowledge or technique.

21. Carry the learning of all important items beyond the point necessary for immediate recall.

22. You must daily pass judgment as to the degree of importance of items that are brought before you, and lay special stress on the permanent fixing of those items that are vital and fundamental.

23. When a given bit of information is clearly of subordinate importance and useful only for the time being, you are warranted in giving to it only sufficient attention to hold it over the time in question.

24. Make the duration of your periods of study long enough to utilize 'warming-up' but not so long as to suffer from weariness or fatigue.

25. When drill or repetition is necessary, distribute over more than one period the time given to a specified learning.

26. When you interrupt work, not only stop at a natural break, but also leave a cue for its quick resumption.

27. After intensive application, especially to new material, pause for a time and let your mind be fallow before taking up anything else.

28. Use various devices to compel yourself to think over your work.

29. Form the habit of working out your own concrete examples of all general rules and principles.

30. Form the habit of mentally reviewing every paragraph as soon as you have read it.

31. Don't hesitate to mark up your own books to make the essential ideas stand out visibly.

32. Whenever your desire is to master material that is at all extensive and complex, make an outline of it. If you also wish to retain this material, commit your outline to memory.

33. In all your work apply your knowledge as much as possible and as soon as possible.

34. Do not hesitate to commit to memory verbatim such materials as definitions of technical terms, formulas, dates and outlines, always provided, of course, that you also understand them.

35. When the material to be learned by heart presents no obvious rational associations, it is perfectly legitimate to invent some artificial scheme for learning and recalling it.

36. In committing to memory a poem, declamation or oration, do not break it up into parts but learn it as a whole.

37. In committing to memory, it is better to read aloud than to read silently and better to read rapidly than slowly.

38. If your work includes attendance at lectures, take a moderate amount of notes during the lectures, using a system of abbreviations, and rewrite these notes daily, amplified into a reasonably compendious outline, organized as suggested in Rule 32.

SUGGESTIONS FOR FURTHER READING

(1) **Breslich, E. R.** Teaching high-school pupils how to study. *School Review*, 20: 1912, 505-515.

(2) **Breslich, E. R.** Supervised study as a means of providing supplementary individual instruction. *Thirteenth Yearbook, Part I, National Society for the Study of Education*, 1914, pp. 32-72. (Bibliography of 19 titles.

(3) **Dearborn, G. V. N.** *How to Learn Easily: a Book for Students, Teachers and Parents.* Boston, 1916.

(4) **Earhart, Lida B.** *Teaching Children to Study.* Boston, 1909. 181 pp.

(5) **Giles, F. M.** Investigation of study-habits of high-school students. *School Review*, 22: 1914, 478-484.

(6) **Hall-Quest, A. L.** The direction of study as the chief aim of the high school. (Chapter X in *The Modern High School*, by **C. H. Johnston** and others).

(7) **Hinsdale, B. A.** *The Art of Study.* New York, 1900, 266 pp.

(8) **Jones, Olivia M.** *Teaching Children to Study; The Group System Applied.* New York, 1910. 193 pp.

(9) **Lunt, F. S.** Some investigations of habits of study, *Jour. of Educational Psychology*, 1: 1910, 344-348.

(10) **McMurry, F. M.** *How to Study and Teaching How to Study.* Boston, 1909. 324 pp.

(11) **Parker, S. C.** *Methods of Teaching in High Schools.* Boston, 1915. 529 pp.

(12) **Reavis, W. C.** The importance of study-program for high-school pupils. *School Review,* 19: 1911, 398-405.

(13) **Rowe, S. H.** The study habit and how to form it. *Education,* 30: 1910, 670-683.

(14) **Ruediger, W. C.** Teaching pupils to study. *Education,* 29: 1909, 437-446.

(15) **Sandwick, R. L.** *How to Study and What to Study.* Boston, 1915. 170 pp.

(16) **Watt, H. J.** *The Economy and Training of Memory.* New York, 1909. 128 pp.

(17) **Wiener, W.** Home-study reform. *School Review,* 20: 1912, 526-531.

www.ingramcontent.com/pod-product-compliance
Lightning Source LLC
Chambersburg PA
CBHW060043040426
42331CB00032B/2252